NOTE TO P

Learning to read is an important skill for al
you can help your child reach. The American Museum of Natural History Easy
Reader program is designed to support you and your child through this process.
Developed by reading specialists, each book in the series includes carefully
selected words and sentence structures to help children advance from beginner
to intermediate to proficient readers.

Here are some tips to keep in mind as you read these books with your child:

First, preview the book together. Read the title. Then look at the cover. Ask your
child, "What is happening on the cover? What do you think this book is about?"

Next, skim through the pages of the book and look at the illustrations. This will
help your child use the illustrations to understand the story.

Then encourage your child to read. If he or she stumbles over words, try some
of these strategies:

- use the pictures as clues
- point out words that are repeated
- sound out difficult words
- break up bigger words into smaller chunks
- use the context to lend meaning

Finally, find out if your child understands what he or she is reading. After you
have finished reading, ask, "What happened in this book?"

Above all, understand that each child learns to read at a different rate. Make
sure to praise your young reader and provide encouragement along the way!

LEVEL 1

Introduce Your Child to Reading
Simple words and simple sentences encourage beginning readers
to sound out words.

LEVEL 2

Your Child Starts to Read
Slightly more difficult words in simple sentences help new readers
build confidence.

LEVEL 3

Your Child Reads with Help
More complex words and sentences and longer text lengths help
young readers reach reading proficiency.

LEVEL 4

Your Child Reads Alone
Practicing difficult words and sentences brings independent readers
to the next level: reading chapter books.

For Max, with love.

—W.P.

Photo credits

Cover/title page: © John Pitcher/iStockphoto.com
Pages 4–6: © M. Watson/Ardea; 7: ©ARCO/U Walz/age fotostock;
8–9: © Stefan Meyers/Ardea; 10–11: © Duncan Usher/Ardea; 12–13: © Tom and Pat Leeson/Ardea;
14: © Angelo Gandolfi/NPL/Minden Pictures; 15: © M. Watson/Ardea; 16–17: © Tom and Pat Leeson/Ardea;
18–19: © Mary Clay/Ardea; 20–21: © Klein-Hubert/Kimball Stock; 22–23: © Eric Dragesco/Ardea;
24: © Frank Parker/age fotostock; 25: © Jeff Lepore/Photo Researchers;
26–27: © Jens Klingebiel/iStockphoto.com; 28: © Denis Pepin/iStockphoto.com;
29: © Duncan Usher/Ardea; 30–31: © Brenda Tharp/Workbook Stock/Getty Images;
32: Photo by Molly Leff © American Museum of Natural History.

STERLING CHILDREN'S BOOKS
New York

An Imprint of Sterling Publishing
387 Park Avenue South
New York, NY 10016

STERLING and the distinctive Sterling logo are registered trademarks of
Sterling Publishing Co., Inc.

Library of Congress Cataloging-in-Publication Data Available

Lot #:
2 4 6 8 10 9 7 5 3 1
04/11
Published by Sterling Publishing Co., Inc.
387 Park Avenue South, New York, NY 10016

www.sterlingpublishing.com/kids

© 2011 by Sterling Publishing Co., Inc., and
The American Museum of Natural History.
Distributed in Canada by Sterling Publishing
c/o Canadian Manda Group, 165 Dufferin Street
Toronto, Ontario, Canada M6K 3H6
Distributed in the United Kingdom by GMC Distribution Services
Castle Place, 166 High Street, Lewes, East Sussex, England BN7 1XU
Distributed in Australia by Capricorn Link (Australia) Pty. Ltd.
P.O. Box 704, Windsor, NSW 2756, Australia

Sterling ISBN 978-1-4027-8564-1 (hardcover)
978-1-4027-7785-1 (paperback)

For information about custom editions, special sales, premium and
corporate purchases, please contact Sterling Special Sales
Department at 800-805-5489 or specialsales@sterlingpublishing.com.

Designed by Amy Wahlfield

FREE ACTIVITIES & PUZZLES ONLINE AT
http://www.sterlingpublishing.com/kids/sterlingeventkits

AMERICAN MUSEUM
OF NATURAL HISTORY
EASY READERS

Wolf Pup

Wendy Pfeffer

STERLING CHILDREN'S BOOKS
New York

It is spring.

A baby wolf is born.

Baby wolves are called pups.

Each pup is very small.

They drink their mother's milk.

A wolf family is called a pack.

Some packs are big.

Other packs are small.

The wolf pup is now six weeks old.

His mother chews food.

She feeds it to her pup.

The pup's parents leave the pack.

They must find more food.

Another wolf stays with the pup.

The mother and father are gone

for many days.

They search for food.

They come back to the den.

The pup licks his mother's face.

It is now summer.

The mother teaches her pup.

He learns how to find food and water.

The pup is getting older.

He runs and plays with another pup.

It is fall.

The pup is six months old.

He can now run with his pack.

The pack must move to find food.

They find a new home.

The wolves in the pack howl.

Owwhoooooo!

The wolf pup hears them.

His head goes up.

His ears lie back.

It is winter.

The wolf pup is nine months old.

He is not a pup anymore.

He is now a young wolf.

The young wolf has large feet
and claws.

They help him run.

He hunts for food with his pack.

The young wolf curls up in a ball.

His fur keeps him warm.

He goes to sleep.

MEET THE EXPERT!

My name is **Neil Duncan**, and I am a biologist. I work for the Division of Vertebrate Zoology at the American Museum of Natural History in New York City. As a collections manager, I get to work with all kinds of animal specimens that have been gathered from around the world.

The natural world has always been a passion of mine, and I have traveled all over the United States to study animals. In California, I researched small forest mammals called fishers and martens; I helped protect endangered shorebirds from human disturbance and from predators in New York; and I have studied many other wildlife species, including fish and whitetail deer.

I received my Bachelor of Science degree in Wildlife and Fisheries Biology from the University of Vermont, and now I am earning my Master's degree from Hofstra University in New York. I am currently studying a species of turtle called the diamondback terrapin. I enjoy learning about diamondback terrapins because they are strong and hardy creatures, and they have managed to survive right near New York City.

If you are interested in biology, one thing you could do is volunteer for a local wildlife organization to learn what kind of animals live in your area. The world of animals is fascinating!